Bald Eagles

Bald Eagles

A Carolrhoda Nature Watch Book

by Charlotte Wilcox

photographs by Jerry Boucher

Carolrhoda Books, Inc. / Minneapolis

This book is dedicated to the children of the victims of the September 11th, 2001, attacks on the United States. May the bald eagle and all it stands for fly free over America forever.
—C. W.

In memory of Patrick Ryan
—J. B.

Text copyright © 2003 by Charlotte Wilcox
Photographs copyright © 2003 by Jerry Boucher, except as noted on p. 48
Illustration on p. 27 by Laura Westlund, copyright © 2003 by Carolrhoda Books, Inc.

Carolrhoda Books, Inc.
A division of Lerner Publishing Group
241 First Avenue North
Minneapolis, MN 55401 U.S.A.

Website address: www.lernerbooks.com

Library of Congress Cataloging-in-Publication Data

Wilcox, Charlotte.
    Bald eagles / by Charlotte Wilcox ; photographs by Jerry Boucher.
        p.   cm.
    A Carolrhoda nature watch book
    Summary: Describes the physical characteristics, life cycle, and behavior of bald eagles, as well as efforts to protect them.
    ISBN: 1–57505–170–2 (lib. bdg. : alk. paper)
    1. Bald eagle—Juvenile literature. [1. Bald eagle. 2. Eagles.]
I. Boucher, Jerry, 1941– ill. II. Title.
QL696.F32 W54 2003
598.9'42—dc21   2001006803

Manufactured in the United States of America
1 2 3 4 5 6 – JR – 08 07 06 05 04 03

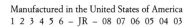

CONTENTS

A SYMBOL OF FREEDOM

In the United States, the bald eagle stands for freedom and strength. A tale from the American Revolution (1775–1783) explains why. A battle took place near a bald eagle nesting spot. The sound of gunfire and the shouts of soldiers scared the birds from their nests. All through the fight, the bald eagles circled overhead. Their sharp screams rose above the battle sounds. To the men below, the eagles sounded like they were crying for freedom.

No one knows for sure if this story is true. But it is true that on June 20, 1782, a design featuring a bald eagle was adopted as the official seal of the United States. Five years later, the bald eagle was made the national emblem. There are eagles on U.S. coins, dollar bills, postage stamps, and military uniforms. Eagles are mascots for sports teams all over the country. The bald eagle is on the official seal of many states, too.

Left: *A lone bald eagle scans its home area for its next meal.*
Above: *The bald eagle, a symbol of American pride and strength, can be found on many official U.S. coins and seals.*

The adult bald eagle's white head makes it easy to spot.

The bald eagle is a uniquely North American bird. When Europeans came to the continent, they had never seen white-headed eagles. Many types of eagles live in Europe, Asia, and Africa. But none of them have the pure white head of the American eagle.

Bald eagles do not have bald heads.

The heads of adult bald eagles are covered with white feathers. The word *bald* means "hairless," but it also means "marked with white." The tail feathers of adult bald eagles are also pure white. This coloring makes the bald eagle one of the world's most recognizable birds.

Despite their beauty, bald eagles have not always been treated with respect and admiration. During the first half of the 1900s, bald eagles almost became **extinct,** or died out, because of the actions of humans. In earlier centuries, hundreds of thousands of bald eagles flew over North America. By the 1960s, only a few thousand remained, mostly in Alaska and western Canada. But after more than 30 years of efforts to save them, bald eagles have made a comeback. In the early 2000s, there are 80,000 to 100,000 bald eagles on the continent. Once again they fly over most of North America.

White tail feathers complete the bald eagle's unique look.

EAGLES AND THEIR WORLD

Eagles are part of a group of birds called **raptors.** Hawks, falcons, owls, and vultures are all members of this group. Raptors, including eagles, are birds of prey. They eat meat. The animals eagles hunt are called **prey.** The term *raptor* comes from the Latin word meaning "to snatch." Bald eagles and most other raptors have strong claws that they use to snatch their food.

There are more than 50 **species,** or types, of eagles in the world. They live on every continent except Antarctica. Only two species, the bald eagle and the golden eagle, live in North America. The bald eagle is the one species of eagle that lives only in North America. Its scientific name is *Haliaeetus leucocephalus.* In Latin this means "sea eagle with a white head."

Bald eagles live only in North America. This captive eagle lives at the University of Minnesota's Raptor Center, in St. Paul, Minnesota.

Bald eagles range from Alaska and Canada to northern Mexico. They live in many kinds of climates, from the hot, dry heat of the Southwest to the icy cold of the North. Most live in Alaska, western Canada, the Pacific Northwest, the Upper Great Lakes region, and Florida. Many live in the Mississippi River valley and along the Atlantic coast.

The golden eagle (below) *and the bald eagle are the only eagles found in the wild in North America. The golden eagle's name comes from the golden feathers on the back of its head.*

The bald eagle's **habitat,** or environment in which it lives, usually consists of open spaces next to forests and water. Fish are a large part of the bald eagle's diet, so open water is important. Bald eagles need forest for shelter. Because they are large birds, bald eagles require plenty of room to take off. They especially thrive along shorelines surrounded by forests. Grasslands with some trees also make a good habitat, as long as there is open water nearby.

Bald eagles prefer to live near open water (left), where they spend much of their time hunting for fish. They also visit grassy areas (below), where they hunt mice and other small animals.

Bald eagles migrate in large groups, traveling up to 200 miles (300 km) a day.

Some groups of bald eagles **migrate,** or move to another area at a certain time of year. They migrate because they need to stay near open water. In warmer climates, like those in the southern United States and northern Mexico and along seacoasts, there is open water all year. Eagles that live in these regions do not migrate. But in other parts of North America, lakes and rivers freeze during winter. Bald eagles in these areas must migrate to warmer locations to find open water. Gathering in groups that may number in the hundreds, they fly as far as 1,200 miles (1,900 km) to their summer or winter homes.

FLIGHT AND FEATHERS

A bald eagle in flight is a spectacular sight. It is one of the largest birds in the sky, and also among the most graceful. Eagles can soar almost motionless, circling in the sky for a long time. An eagle's body is streamlined like an airplane, so it glides through the air with ease.

Large, powerful wings help bald eagles fly at fantastic speeds. The wingspan, or distance between outstretched wing tips, of an average male bald eagle is 6.5 feet (2.0 m). Female bald eagles, like all female raptors, are bigger than males. The wingspan of an average female is 7.5 feet (2.3 m). In level flight, these big wings can push the bald eagle to nearly 65 miles per hour (105 km/h).

In a dive, a bald eagle can reach speeds well over 100 miles per hour (160 km/h). They have been seen at elevations of 10,000 feet (3,000 m). That's almost 2 miles (3 km) high! Sometimes eagles fly so high they can't be seen from the ground.

Bald eagles' bodies are large compared to the bodies of most other birds, but they don't weigh very much. An average bald eagle's body length from head to tail is about 3 feet (1 m), but a full-grown female weighs only 9 to 15 pounds (4–6.8 kg). Males weigh a little less—from 7 to 12 pounds (3–5.4 kg). A 3-foot-tall (1-m-tall) person weighs about 40 pounds (almost 20 kg). Like most birds, eagles have hollow bones, making them lightweight. The lighter a bird is, the less work it has to do to stay in the air.

A full-grown bald eagle like this one can spread its wings 6.5 feet (2.0 m) or more.

These two young bald eagles have soft, downy feathers. Adults have a coat of long, smooth feathers (**inset**) *that help them to fly.*

A bald eagle's feathers are very important for flying and keeping the eagle warm and dry. The bird has a set of long, outer feathers that are smooth, allowing it to glide through the air. It also has a layer of fluffy feathers close to its skin that keep it warm.

Bald eagles spend a lot of time diving for fish in cold water. Just as wet clothes won't keep you warm, wet feathers cannot keep an eagle warm. Glands above the eagle's tail produce an oil that keeps water from soaking through the feathers. An eagle scratches the oil glands with its beak to push the oil out. Then it uses its beak to spread the oil over its feathers in an action called **preening.** Bald eagles may spend hours at a time preening and arranging their feathers.

An eagle snatches at a fish. Eagles often catch their food in water, so they have to spend a lot of time preening their feathers to keep them waterproof.

This eagle is just getting started on its meal.

FINDING FOOD

Bald eagles' favorite food is fish, but they will eat anything they can find. They also hunt small animals, such as rabbits, mice, and birds. They are good hunters, but only hunt when they have to. Bald eagles are always on the lookout for an easy meal, and will often steal food from other birds, even other bald eagles. During winter or when migrating, bald eagles usually search for food in small groups.

In western North America, eagles eat mostly salmon. Great numbers of these large fish live in the rivers of the West. An adult bald eagle may eat several fish in a day.

Salmon are easiest to hunt during the fall and early winter, when they move from the ocean to streams in order to reproduce. Every November, between 3,000 and 4,000 bald eagles travel to the Chilkat River in Alaska to feast on salmon. This yearly event is the largest gathering of bald eagles in the world.

Bald eagles also eat **carrion,** or rotting meat. Carrion may be animals that have been killed by cars, people, or other animals, or that have died naturally. It may be the remains of livestock from farms or ranches. Bald eagles almost never kill farm animals. But they will eat them if they find them dead.

The bald eagle's favorite food is fish, including salmon.

This group of eagles is hunting for fish. Eagles spend much of their day in search of food.

During migration season, bald eagles gather in groups. They seem to follow the best hunters. When one bald eagle finds something to eat, others will soon gather. Many groups may join together to form larger groups of hundreds or even thousands of eagles. Even when migrating, eagles spend much of their time searching for food.

Excellent eyesight helps the bald eagle to be a great hunter. Scientists think that eagles may have the best eyesight of all creatures. Their vision is many times sharper than a human's. A bald eagle can spot a small animal or fish from more than 1 mile (over 1 km) away! The eagle's powerful vision comes from the many special cells in its eyes called **cones.** These cells allow eyes to see colors and details. Humans have cones in their eyes, but an eagle has many thousands more.

Bald eagles have built-in protection for their eyes. They have heavy eyebrows that come down over their eyes. Each eye also has two eyelids. Underneath each outer eyelid is a second, very thin eyelid that blinks every few seconds. Eagles can see through this inner eyelid. It helps keep dirt and dust out of their eyes.

The bald eagle depends on its excellent eyesight for hunting.

Bald eagles can turn their heads almost all the way around to see what's behind them.

Bald eagles have a wide range of vision. While humans can see only what's in front of them, bald eagles have large eyes that see both to the front and to the side. But bald eagles cannot move their eyes inside their sockets the way people can. When looking far to the side, a bald eagle must turn its whole head. Bald eagles have very flexible necks, however, and they can turn their heads almost all the way around and upside down. This flexibility allows eagles to see behind them without turning their bodies.

A bald eagle's wings play an important part in capturing prey. In a dive, the wings act as brakes. When hunting, an eagle dives at lightning speed from high in the sky. Just before reaching its prey, the eagle spreads its wings wide and pushes its feet forward. Its swift flight comes almost to a stop. Quickly, the bald eagle's sharp claws, called **talons,** snatch the prey.

Occasionally the eagle will go too deep into the water. Its feathers may get so wet that it cannot fly. When this happens, the eagle has to swim to shore. But usually the eagle is in the air again in a split second, holding its meal in its talons. Bald eagles have four toes, with a sharp talon on each. The toes are long—nearly 6 inches (15 cm) long when fully stretched out. Three toes face forward and one backward. This placement helps the bald eagle hold on to its prey, similar to the way a human thumb and fingers grip objects. Bald eagles can carry food while flying for several miles (several km).

Bald eagles have four toes on each foot, and each toe has a long, sharp claw for grasping prey. The skin on the bottom of the eagle's foot is rough, like sandpaper, to keep hold of slippery fish.

Bald eagles also use their powerful, hooked beaks to hold and tear food. They have mouths that open very wide. Having a big mouth is necessary because bald eagles do not chew their food. They eat small fish whole. They use their beaks and talons to tear larger prey into mouth-sized pieces. Bald eagles are not fussy eaters. They eat their prey's bones, teeth, feathers, or fur along with its meat.

Left: *An eagle does not use its sharp beak as a weapon. Instead, the beak is used for tearing captured prey into bite-sized pieces.*
Right: *This bald eagle has successfully snatched a fish from the water. The eagle's strong feet will hold the struggling fish while the bird finds a safe place to land and eat.*

Adult bald eagles eat up to 1 pound (0.5 kg) of food a day.

When a bald eagle swallows, the food goes into a pouch called a **crop**. The food is softened in the crop before it is digested. Bald eagles sometimes store extra food in their crops. If they eat more than they need at one meal, they can save the food for later. When food is scarce, an adult can store 2 pounds (1 kg) or more of food in its crop for a short time.

Like all birds, bald eagles have stomachs with two parts. The first part of the stomach is small and soft, and holds strong acids that break down food. The second part is called the **gizzard.** The gizzard is larger than the first part of the stomach. It traps things the eagle cannot digest, such as bone chips, feathers, or fur. The gizzard has walls made of hard muscles that roll these unusable parts into **pellets,** or hard balls, that the eagle throws up and spits out.

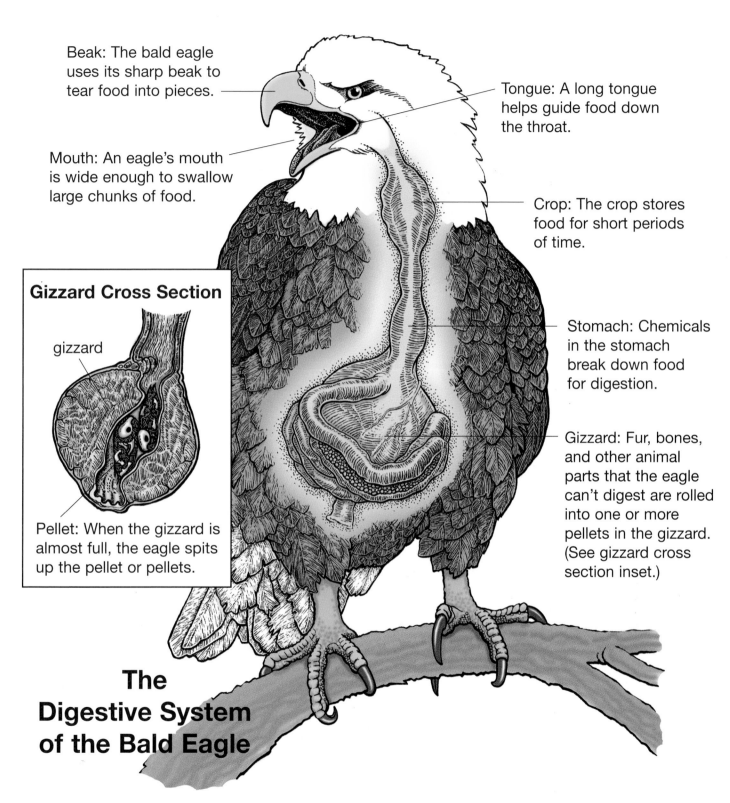

Beak: The bald eagle uses its sharp beak to tear food into pieces.

Mouth: An eagle's mouth is wide enough to swallow large chunks of food.

Tongue: A long tongue helps guide food down the throat.

Crop: The crop stores food for short periods of time.

Stomach: Chemicals in the stomach break down food for digestion.

Gizzard: Fur, bones, and other animal parts that the eagle can't digest are rolled into one or more pellets in the gizzard. (See gizzard cross section inset.)

Gizzard Cross Section

gizzard

Pellet: When the gizzard is almost full, the eagle spits up the pellet or pellets.

The Digestive System of the Bald Eagle

27

LIFE CYCLE

When bald eagles are 4 to 6 years old, they choose a mate. When choosing mates, eagles play together to get to know one another. They call to each other and chase one another through the air. Two eagles sometimes lock talons with each other in midair. Once a pair mates, they usually stay together until one of them dies. Together, they claim a **territory,** or area in which they live. This area often remains their home for life. The couple may build several nests in their territory.

Bald eagle pairs start nesting in the fall in southern climates. Scientists think eagles nest during this time because the hot summer heat is dangerous to baby eagles. In colder regions, nesting does not start until January or February. Eagles that have nested before often return to and repair their old nest. Newly mated couples build a new nest. They will live in this nest for the next 6 months.

Bald eagles mate for life. When one mate dies, the surviving mate finds a new partner.

Nests are almost always located in a tree near open water. The tree must have branches large enough to hold up a huge nest. Bald eagles often pick the tallest tree around, so they will have a good view. They do not like deep forest because they need a clear flight path to the nest. But they do not want a tree that is out in the open, either. They need privacy to raise their young. Bald eagles especially like evergreen trees, such as fir, spruce, or pine. These trees do not lose their needles, so they provide good shelter all year round.

Bald eagles build some of the biggest nests in the bird world. They are huge structures, 5 to 8 feet (about 2 m) wide, high in a tree. Scientists have found nests weighing nearly 4,000 pounds (1,800 kg). Sometimes nests get so big that they break the tree branches and crash to the ground.

The female bald eagle often does most of the building, with some help from the male. The nest is made from sticks, woven together between strong branches below the top of the tree. Inside, it has a soft bed of grass, weeds, moss, or cornstalks. A bald eagle pair can build a nest 3 feet (1 m) deep in about 4 days.

Top: *Bald eagles make some of the world's largest nests.*
Bottom: *Eagles weave the nest tightly into a tree, so it doesn't fall out in stormy weather.*

Left: *A bald eagle warns an intruder to stay away from its nest.*
Below: *An eagle keeps an eye out for other animals that might try to steal its eggs.*

When several pairs nest in the same area, they usually build their nests 1 mile or more (over 1 km) away from each other. To protect their young, the parents chase other eagles out of their territory.

Bald eagles begin life as cream-colored eggs, 2 to 3 inches (5–8 cm) long. The female lays one to three eggs, each a few days apart. Both parents spend time keeping the eggs warm. They use their beaks to turn the eggs over about once each hour, day and night. Turning the eggs keeps them from getting too cold or too warm on one side. During this period, at least one parent stays in the nest at all times. Often, the other one will keep guard nearby. When both are in the nest, they look in opposite directions, watching for danger from all sides.

After 34 to 38 days, the baby eagles, or **eaglets,** are ready to hatch. They use a special bump on top of their beaks, called an **egg tooth,** to break the eggshell. The eaglets hatch a few days apart, in the order the eggs were laid. Each weighs almost 3 ounces (90 g) when it hatches. They are covered with soft, gray feathers called **down.**

Breaking out of the shell is hard work for the eaglets. It may take up to 2 days. When they finally appear, the eaglets are exhausted and soaking wet. They spend their first day sleeping underneath their parents. By the next day, they are dry, wide awake, and very hungry. The young eagles soon learn to cry and beg for food. For the next 3 months, the parents spend most of their time feeding the eaglets.

Left: *Bald eagle eggs*
Above: *A baby bald eagle*

The male eagle does most of the hunting and brings food back to the nest. The female then feeds the food to the eaglets. At least one of the eaglets' parents stands guard at the nest during this time, keeping an eye out for danger.

Eaglets grow surprisingly fast. They may eat as much as or more than an adult. They can put on 1 pound (0.5 kg) of weight every 4 or 5 days. At 1 month old, they may be 1 foot (0.3 m) tall and they can stand up. About this time, they begin to lose their fluffy down. The sturdy, brown-black feathers that are necessary for flying begin to grow in.

At 10 to 12 weeks, the eaglets are ready to learn to fly. The parents gradually bring less food to the nest. The eaglets begin to lose their baby fat. They start to flap their wings in the wind. They practice hunting by attacking insects or bone scraps in the nest. Parents may tease the eaglets by bringing pieces of food near the nest, then flying off with them.

Eaglets grow very fast. Within 4 months of hatching, they grow to the size of their parents.

This young bald eagle will face many dangers in its first year.

The young bald eagles' first flight can be a dangerous one. They start from the edge of the nest, often gliding to the ground on the wind. They may fly to a nearby branch. Sometimes the eaglets fall to the ground. Most get up and try again, but some do not. An eagle that cannot fly has no chance of surviving in the wild.

When the young eagles are able to fly, they can learn to hunt. The family stays together for a few more weeks so the parents can teach the young birds. For a while, parents still give the young eagles food when they beg. But little by little, the young eagles learn to feed themselves. By the time they leave their parents at 3 or 4 months, they weigh about 10 pounds (over 4 kg). They are the size of their parents, but they have much to learn.

Less than half of all bald eagles survive their first year. They may starve because they cannot find or catch enough food. They may freeze because they cannot find good shelter in bad weather. Sometimes their lack of experience with people can cause problems. They may get caught in traps or even shot, though shooting bald eagles is illegal. More than three-fourths of all bald eagles may die before they reach breeding age. Only those that become strong and skillful hunters will live long.

The speckled feathers of the eagle on the left show that this bird has not yet reached adulthood. If it survives its first 5 years, the eagle will have the same white head and tail and dark body as the eagle on the right.

Young eagles that do survive begin to look more like adults. This occurs through a process called **molting,** during which eagles lose their old feathers and grow new ones. A young eagle has mostly brown or brown-black feathers, with lighter feathers on the underside of its wings. As the eagle grows older, it loses its darker feathers and grows feathers that are speckled with white and dark brown. Eventually, the eagle sheds these speckled feathers, too. The new head and tail feathers that grow back are lighter

each time the eagle molts. They are pure white when the bird is about 5 years of age. At the same time, the feathers on the eagle's wings and body get darker, until they are almost black.

When eagles are old enough to breed, they choose mates just as their parents did. The pairs nest, hatch eggs, and raise young. After the nesting season, many adult bald eagles leave their nests and join larger groups for the rest of the year. They stay in these groups to travel, look for food, or rest.

When a bald eagle is not hunting for food, traveling, or caring for its young, it spends much of each day on a **perch.** A perch is a place where birds sit during the day. Bald eagles prefer large branches in tall trees overlooking a good hunting or fishing spot. They especially like perches in standing dead trees, called snags. These give a good view because snags do not have leaves or needles. Sometimes bald eagles use power lines, power poles, tall rocks, or cliffs as perches. During the nesting season, they choose a perch near the nest.

From their perches, bald eagles scan the ground or nearby water for prey. After feeding, they return to the perches to watch again. Sometimes they carry food there to eat it. While on a perch, they may preen, dry their feathers in the sun, or simply rest.

Bald eagles will often perch for hours at a time.

At night, bald eagles gather in groups to **roost.** The place where they gather at night is also called a roost. It is usually in a quieter, more protected area than a perch. For roosting, bald eagles like trees with plenty of leaves or long needles for shelter. They leave the roost when it begins to get light in the morning, and they return at sunset. They fly to the roost during the day if bad weather hits. The same eagles often return to a favorite roost year after year.

Bald eagles live long lives for birds. Those that survive their early years may live 20 years or longer.

Bald eagles often roost in groups.

36

Only Native Americans are allowed to own bald eagle feathers. The United States government keeps careful track of all bald eagle feathers found in the wild.

BALD EAGLES AND PEOPLE

Numerous Native American groups consider the bald eagle a very special creature. They prize eagle feathers for religious rituals. The feathers are considered special gifts that are handed down from one generation to another. For centuries, Native Americans held special religious hunts to kill bald eagles for their feathers.

When Europeans arrived in North America, they were struck by the bald eagle's uncommon beauty. But they did not always share the Native Americans' respect for the birds. Some European settlers believed that bald eagles were pests. Some thought the eagles were eating too many fish. Others thought that bald eagles killed farm animals such as lambs and chickens. Even though bald eagles rarely kill farm animals, many farmers and ranchers shot bald eagles when they had the chance.

A bald eagle skull. Bald eagles nearly died out in the 1900s.

By the early 1900s, bald eagles were dying out in the United States. In 1940, the U.S. Congress passed the Bald Eagle Protection Act, making it a crime to harm bald eagles.

Then, in 1947, a new danger appeared. It was DDT, a chemical used to kill insects. In the 1950s and 1960s, DDT was sprayed on fields and shorelines all across North America to kill mosquitoes and other pests. The chemical washed into lakes and rivers. It soaked into plants, insects, and fish living in the waters. When birds ate the plants, insects, or fish, they ate DDT as well.

Soon after people started using DDT,

scientists began to notice that many birds were raising fewer and fewer young. At first, no one knew why. Then scientists discovered that many birds were laying eggs with very thin shells. The shells were breaking before the young birds were ready to hatch. Because new birds were not hatching, many bird species soon were **endangered,** or in danger of becoming extinct. By 1965, there were only about 3,700 bald eagles left in North America, even though there had once been hundreds of thousands of them. Only a few hundred of these remaining eagles were breeding adults.

When the chemical DDT poisoned North American waters, many animals were affected, including the bald eagle.

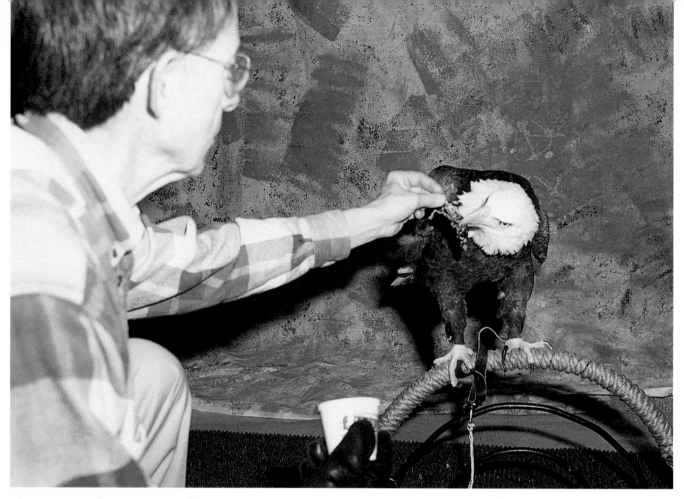

A scientist at the University of Minnesota's Raptor Center feeds an injured bald eagle. Many programs around the country take in wounded bald eagles and nurse them back to health.

In 1967, the U.S. government declared bald eagles in the southern United States to be endangered. In most of the rest of the United States, bald eagles were declared endangered in 1978. The bald eagle population was considered safe only in Alaska and Canada.

In the late 1960s, scientists finally figured out that DDT was causing the thin eggshells. Canada banned the use of DDT in 1970, and the United States banned it in 1972. In 1973, scientists began working to help bald eagles. One way they did this was by stealing their babies! Scientists knew that a pair of eagles rarely raises more than two eaglets each year. They watched the nests of breeding adult eagles. After the eggs hatched, workers looked for nests with more than two babies. When they found one, they took the extra eaglet out.

Sometimes scientists put the eaglets in a nest where some or all of the eggs did not hatch. The new parents usually adopted the eaglets and raised them as their own. More often, humans raised the eaglets themselves. Workers cared for the eaglets until they were ready to fly.

From the 1970s to the 1990s, eaglets were gathered from northern states such as Alaska, Minnesota, and Wisconsin. They were sent to areas where the bald eagle population had died out. This program was a huge success. It worked so well that scientists discontinued it in the mid-1990s. The bald eagle population had grown so much that the program wasn't necessary anymore.

Bald eagles still get help from humans. Scientists keep track of where the eagles nest and where they go. They capture bald eagles without harming them. The scientists examine the eagles carefully. They record their size, age, and health. Wildlife workers glue a radio transmitter to the bald eagle's tail. Workers also attach color-coded plastic tags to the eagles' wings. The wing tags make it easy for scientists to tell where eagles have been before.

After the transmitters and tags are in place, the eagles are set free. The transmitter sends out radio signals to receivers on the ground or in aircraft. They help scientists learn about bald eagles' habits and travels. They even help scientists find eagles that have died. People have been arrested for shooting eagles because transmitters led law officers to the eagles' bodies.

A transmitter like this one is attached to an eagle's tail. The transmitter sends radio signals that scientists can use to track the eagle's movements.

In 1995, the U.S. government moved the bald eagle from the endangered species list to the threatened species list. A threatened animal's situation is not as serious as an endangered animal's, but threatened animals still need to be protected. Eagle populations increased greatly in the late 1990s. But bald eagles still face dangers. In the 1990s and early 2000s, dozens of bald eagles in the southeastern United States died from a mysterious illness. Also, bald eagles that nest around the shores of the Great Lakes do not have as many eaglets as eagles in other parts of the country have. No one knows why.

In other regions, buildings are being constructed in bald eagles' habitat. When this happens, the eagles must move away. But eagles prefer to live near the place where they grew up. When chased out of their home territory, they look for another territory close by. If too many eagles are living in one area, there may not be enough food to go around.

Losing their habitat to humans is still a threat to many bald eagles. These eagles live close enough to humans to hunt for food in a garbage dump.

Bald eagles circle over the Mississippi River near Guttenberg, Iowa.

Native Americans still value bald eagles and their feathers. But they no longer hunt the birds. It is illegal for anyone to kill or capture bald eagles. Unless you are a Native American, it is illegal to keep any part of a bald eagle, including a feather, even if it is found on the ground.

Instead of hunting eagles, Native Americans get eagle feathers from the National Eagle Repository in Denver, Colorado. This is where park rangers and wildlife workers send dead eagles when they find them. This center is part of the U.S. Fish and Wildlife Service. The eagles brought there may have been electrocuted, shot, or hit by a car, or died of illness. The center receives about 900 dead eagles each year.

Only Native Americans may get feathers from the National Eagle Repository. They may use them only for religious purposes. They cannot give the feathers away to anyone who is not Native American. But they can pass the feathers down from one generation to the next.

Bald eagles once again range over most of North America. They can be found in every American state and Canadian province, from California to Nova Scotia. Among the best places to see bald eagles are Alaska and British Columbia. Another good place is the northern Mississippi River valley. Up to 5,000 bald eagles spend the winter along the Mississippi River in Minnesota, Wisconsin, Iowa, and Ilinois.

A good time to see bald eagles is in the fall and early winter. This is the time when eagles gather around open water, especially rivers where salmon are present.

During nesting season, people should not disturb bald eagles. Most adult bald eagles will fly away if a human gets too close to their nest. The parents may stay away so long that their eggs or eaglets may get too cold and die.

Many zoos and wildlife parks also keep bald eagles for viewing by the public. These are usually birds that have been hurt and cannot be sent back to the wild. Eagles that were raised by humans and learned to trust them also cannot return to the wild. Their lack of fear for humans would bring them into too much danger. Besides, eagles raised to trust humans often do not get along with other eagles.

Bald eagles have inspired Americans for hundreds of years. In the 2000s, they are inspiring people in a new way. Bald eagles faced many dangers, but with help, they found new ways to prosper. For this century, they are a symbol of more than freedom. They are also a symbol of strength, because they have survived dangers to fill the skies of North America once again.

GLOSSARY

carrion: rotting meat

cone: a kind of cell in an eagle's eye that allows the bird to see colors and details

crop: the pouch in which a bird stores and softens food

down: soft, fluffy feathers

eaglet: a young eagle

egg tooth: a bump on the top of a baby bird's beak, which the bird uses to break through its eggshell

endangered: in danger of dying out

extinct: having died out

gizzard: the hard, muscular, second part of a bird's stomach

habitat: the place and conditions in which an animal naturally lives

migrate: to move to another area at a certain time of year

molt: to shed old feathers and grow new ones

pellet: a small, hard ball. An eagle's gizzard rolls fur, feathers, and bone chips into pellets that the eagle can throw up.

perch: a place where birds sit and rest during the day, usually up high; also, to sit or rest on a perch

preen: to use a beak to clean, oil, and arrange feathers. Birds preen themselves and their young, and sometimes other adult birds.

prey: an animal that is hunted and eaten; also, the act of hunting and eating an animal

raptor: a meat-eating bird

roost: a place where birds spend the night; also, to perch for the night

species: a type of animal or plant. Members of the same species can mate and produce young.

talon: a sharp claw of a bird of prey

territory: an area claimed as an eagle's home and defended from other animals

INDEX

ABOUT THE AUTHOR

Charlotte Wilcox is a freelance writer and graphic designer. She has written more than 40 nonfiction books for children and young adults, including the award-winning titles *Mummies & Their Mysteries* and *Mummies, Bones, & Body Parts,* published by Carolrhoda Books, Inc. Charlotte has also produced travel guides, trade publications, and educational materials. She lives and works on the farm where she grew up, near Minnesota's St. Croix River. From her office window she can watch the many bald eagles that glide over the farm and stop to perch in the trees around the barnyard.

ABOUT THE PHOTOGRAPHER

Jerry Boucher has been a professional photographer for more than 30 years. Currently most of his photography goes into tourism guides, which he produces through his company, Schoolhouse Productions. Jerry has teamed with Charlotte Wilcox on two other titles for Carolrhoda Books: *Trash!* and *Powerhouse: Inside a Nuclear Power Plant.* Jerry's photography has also appeared in the Carolrhoda titles *Fire Truck Nuts and Bolts* and *Flush! Treating Wastewater.* Jerry and his wife Elaine live in Amery, Wisconsin.

PHOTO ACKNOWLEDGEMENTS

All photos courtesy of Jerry Boucher, except: © Lynn M. Stone, front cover, pp. 18, 26, 42, 45; © Natalie Fobes, p. 19; © The Raptor Center, University of Minnesota, pp. 21, 37, 41; © Jeffrey Rich, Nature Photography, p. 25; © State of Minnesota, Department of Natural Resources, p. 31 (left); © D. Ellis/Visuals Unlimited, p. 31 (right).